August, 1995

# THE DOORS OF SAN MIGUEL DE ALLENDE

# THE DOORS OF SAN MIGUEL DE ALLENDE

*Robert de Gast*

POMEGRANATE ARTBOOKS   SAN FRANCISCO

*For Evelyn*

4

Published by Pomegranate Artbooks
Box 6099, Rohnert Park, California 94927

© 1994 Robert de Gast

Library of Congress Cataloging-in-Publication Data
de Gast, Robert, 1936–
     The doors of San Miguel de Allende / Robert de Gast. —1st ed.
          p.     cm.
     ISBN 1-56640-990-X : $16.95
     1. Doors—Mexico—San Miguel de Allende—Pictorial works. 1. San Miguel de Allende (Mexico)—Buildings, structures, etc.     I. Title.
NA3010.D35   1994
721' .822 ' 097241—dc20                                                    94–20415
                                                                                    CIP

Designed by Bonnie Smetts Design

First Edition

Printed in Korea

There are many places—probably dozens—called San Miguel in Hispanic America. The former Spanish territories now known as Texas, California, Arizona and New Mexico all have a San Miguel, and every country in South and Central America boasts one or more. But, for most Americans, San Miguel means San Miguel de Allende, a small town near the geographic center of Mexico in the state of Guanajuato. For the past half century it has drawn a growing group of expatriates.

Casually sophisticated, intellectually stimulating and architecturally beautiful,

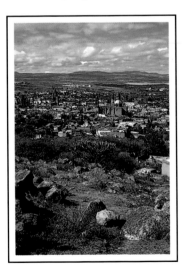

San Miguel de Allende attracts thousands of visitors each year. Mexican tourists pay homage to its history, since the town occupies a place in Mexico's past much as Boston or Philadelphia does in the history of the United States. Americans and Canadians are enamored of its nearly flawless climate, with sunny days and cool nights year round. It is dry most of the year, but in summer, late afternoon rain showers turn the surrounding countryside into a lush, green landscape.

San Miguel de Allende lies on the edge of the Bajío, Mexico's bread basket. "Bajío" means "low place," which would seem to be a strange designation for an area nearly a mile above sea level, but the surrounding mountains account for it. The town nestles at 6,000 feet against the lower slopes of the Hill of Moctezuma, with its western horizon dominated by the craggy 9,000-foot Guanajuato Mountains, thirty miles away.

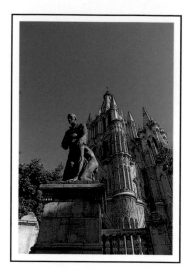

Most of San Miguel de Allende's 600-square-mile area is sparsely settled. Eighty thousand people, two-thirds of the population, live in the barrios and burgeoning subdivisions within the actual town of some forty square miles. The town's center, the single square mile of the Historic District, houses about 5,000 residents. From almost any street in this ancient village, inhabitants and tourists may look out at the surrounding countryside and reach it on foot.

San Miguel de Allende is one of Mexico's oldest towns. At some time between 1538 and 1542—less than half a century after Columbus's first voyage to the Americas and not two decades since the conquest of Mexico—Fray Juan, a Franciscan priest, established a settlement he named San Miguel de Chichimecas for his patron saint Michael and the dominant Indian tribe. Fray Juan built a chapel with a thatched roof and some huts several miles west of the present town center on the banks of a small river, Rio Laja. Now partially dammed and useful as the source of the Presa, or reservoir, the river proved an unreliable water supply for the early settlement. So, Fray Juan's French successor, Fray Bernardo Cossin, rebuilt the settlement near the spring called El Chorro del Cerro ("The Spurt of the Hill"), which still serves the town today. The priests taught the Indians European techniques of weaving and encouraged other indigenous crafts, thereby establishing a tradition of artistic sensibility and craftsmanship still evident in today's population.

At about the same time that San Miguel was established, silver was discovered in the mountains near Guanajuato and Zacatecas, and the settlement found itself on the route between the mountains and Mexico City. As a result, it grew quickly in size and wealth and became known as San Miguel el Grande, the largest town in Mexico named after St. Michael. In the flatter, lower section of town, streets were laid out according to the typical Spanish grid pattern, while roads and alleys in the higher, hillier parts obeyed the dictates of terrain. Many of the substantial buildings, residences, churches and monasteries erected during this period still survive. Silver mining was exhausted after about one hundred years of exploitation, and San Miguel el Grande, no longer so grand, became a quiet, backwater town.

By the beginning of the nineteenth century there was widespread unrest in Mexico: the country was ready to be freed of Spanish control. In 1810 revolution began in earnest, led by Miguel Hidalgo, a priest from the nearby town of Dolores, and Ignacio Allende, the officer in charge of the San Miguel royal regiment. When the rebels failed, both men were captured and later beheaded. Today, they are revered as the "fathers of the revolution" that finally succeeded in 1821.

Shortly after the revolution, San Miguel el Grande was renamed San Miguel de Allende, in honor of its most famous citizen. In the early 1900s it was declared a national monument so that its unique Spanish Colonial buildings would be protected from exterior change. (In 1982 another declaration created a historical zone of sixty-eight blocks and tightened the protective regulations.)

In 1938 American artist Stirling Dickenson wandered upon San Miguel and was taken by its well-preserved architecture and benign climate. He decided to make the town his home and, after World War II, helped found an art school there, now called the Instituto Allende. Another art academy, the Centro Cultural Ignacio Ramírez, was founded a decade later in a glorious former nunnery called La Concepción. The schools attracted Mexican and foreign artists, many of whom stayed after finishing their studies. Over the following decades, San Miguel developed into an important cultural center, without losing its traditional charm.

Today the cultural scene remains lively. There are classes and workshops on a wide range of subjects including poetry, scriptwriting, sculpting, painting, yoga and Spanish. There is a never-ending season of plays, concerts and exhibitions, and the town boasts nearly a dozen art galleries. Many of these activities are offered in English for San Miguel's substantial population of *norteamericano* expatriates.

San Miguel is not an artificial, sanitized Colonial Williamsburg. It is a real, viable and vibrant community that would manage very well without the influx of tourists and immigrants. While it has a number of first-class hotels and restau-

rants, luxurious gift shops and other landmarks indicative of its status as a fashionable tourist destination, there are lumberyards next to the fancy eateries and hardware stores adjoining the hotels, and the milk (unpasteurized) and firewood (unseasoned) are still delivered by burro door-to-door.

San Miguel's Historic District is centered on the Plaza de Allende, a small, formal square usually called the Jardín. Between 1900 and 1910 the Jardín was transformed from a flat, featureless and dusty parade ground into a formal garden with iron benches, sculpted laurel trees and a bandstand in the middle. Around the four sides of the Jardín are some of the grandest buildings in San Miguel: Ignacio Allende's birthplace, the mansion of the Counts of Canal and the splendid parish church, La Parroquia. Although its style has been described as "fake Gothic" and "Disneyesque," this landmark church instantly identifies San Miguel de Allende, just as the Eiffel Tower announces Paris.

The Jardín is much more than the geographic center of town. It is its social center, both for the San Miguelenses and for the foreign community. Nearly everything is measured and described by its proximity to the Jardín. Here one meets friends, has one's shoes shined, buys the newspaper. Here the festivals are celebrated and the fireworks ignited. On weekend evenings, the Jardín hosts the endless *paseo,* with young people of both sexes parading around the plaza, giggling and flirting, while their elders and the younger children watch the proceedings from the somewhat uncomfortable benches.

The Historic District can be circumnavigated easily in an hour's walk; walking the dozens of uneven, bumpy stone streets within it is another matter.

Appropriate footwear helps one to stay balanced but does not alleviate the confusion of finding one's way. Sometimes a street changes its name almost every block. (Extensions to the original streets were given new and different names, and commemorations of current heroes required new names for existing streets.) The confusion is compounded where some streets have received new names but their old names are still embedded in the stucco walls of street corners. The visitor is further baffled by signs—left over from an earlier locating scheme—on nearly every street corner reading "Manzana" with a number. Newcomers find themselves on the corner of Manzana and Manzana, and it doesn't help to know that "manzana" means both "apple" and "block."

The buildings in the Historic District are made of adobe, brick, rubble stone usually covered with stucco, or solid hewn rock. The roofs are flat. This particular type of construction, with huge, heavy, horizontal timbers embedded in parapeted masonry walls to support a cement or dirt roof, can be traced to Moorish origin, but the method was also developed independently by several groups of Native Americans and was well established in Mexico when the Spaniards arrived. The houses are generally one story high, except for the two-story grand mansions of the wealthy and powerful, which appear even higher since their ceilings often reach from ten to twenty feet.

The Spanish Colonial design typical of San Miguel's residences serves a number of architectural and social purposes. The structure has all the elements of a fortress, not only defeating the sun's heat but also assuring privacy, especially on the second floor. The dwellings developed as a series of independent rooms, first linked end-to-end and eventually added at right angles to form an L, U or rectangle with an inner courtyard. Most rooms open to the courtyard only, and a single, modest doorway marks the entrance to the compound. This door is invariably closed for privacy,

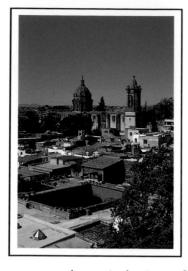

and the patient pedestrian can expect only the merest glimpse—as the door is opened to admit a visitor or to clean the sidewalks—of the splendor or chaos behind it.

Traditionally, doors in Mexico were made of wood, and it wasn't until the mid 1900s that metal doors became the popular choice in new home construction. In San Miguel's Historic District, the metal door is a rarity. The huge doors of the more elaborate mansions, able to admit horse and carriage, are wooden, often with a smaller door set in to accommodate entrance for a single person. Except for the narrowest doors, single pieces of wood were not sufficiently wide to cover the entryway, so vertical planks were fastened together with horizontal crosspieces, nailed or, more recently, screwed in place. Sometimes the nails were held in a clinched position and prevented from pulling through by bosses, large washers that lend themselves to decoration. Clinching nails, now viewed as crude, were used in the finest construction.

The area around a door is usually painted a different color. Even if the doorjambs and lintels are not made of separate material but are self-edged continuations of the walls, contrasting colors or textures are introduced.

A mail slot is frequently only a narrow slit in a door. It may be made of brass or stamped metal and marked "Cartas," "Correo" or "Buzon." Doorknockers are popular and are often cast in whimsical animal shapes, hands or fists. Strings to activate doorbells or, increasingly, buttons for electric bells are located high enough so that little schoolchildren will not be able to act on their temptations. Strings streaming from some doorways facilitate the opening, without a key, of the door from outside. When more security is required, it is a simple matter to retrieve the string of the sliding bolt on the inside. Doorknobs are a rarity, although doorpulls abound.

Many doors display small signs that say "Somos Católicos" ("We are Catholics") to try to forestall the efforts of increasingly active Protestant missionaries. Other cryptic chalk signs with letters or numbers refer to certain census data that the municipal government tries to collect on sizes of households or water and sewage access.

It is fair to say that San Miguel is not quite as pretty as it once was. Antennas, pole-mounted transformers and other evidence of technological progress have marred the once breathtaking vistas. Rather than chisel channels for wires and cables in the stone and stuccoed brick buildings, installers have cavalierly and carelessly draped them around windows, roofs and doors.

Still, San Miguel de Allende is one of the most beautiful towns in Mexico. And, certainly, part of its charm stems from the astonishing variety and lively beauty of its doors.

# THE PHOTOGRAPHS

It is not a coincidence that architectural treasures are remembered for their entrances. Like many people, I have been fascinated with doors for a long time, and when I first visited San Miguel de Allende in 1987 I instantly fell in love with the town, not least because of its diverse assortment of doors. During my short stay, I took a number of photographs, mostly of doors, and those pictures helped keep my memory of San Miguel acutely alive.

In the winter of 1992, I returned to San Miguel to begin work on this book. It seemed a simple matter to come up with a plan of action: walk the streets and photograph what caught my eye. If I walked long enough and tried hard enough, I'd soon have a collection of interesting pictures.

As it turned out, during my first month's stay in January, a traditionally dry month, it rained nearly every day thanks to wild changes in the location of the El Niño current. While I wanted to photograph some doors in the shade or on days without sun, working in the rain has never been appealing to me or productive. So I decided to begin my project by making notes about likely subjects and returning to those locations when light and weather served. However, when I returned to an address when conditions seemed appropriate, I found myself wondering what on Earth had induced me to choose that door for a subject. The direction a door faced and the time of day—together with surprise and serendipity—all affected my reaction to each door. So when the weather began to cooperate in February I meandered through the same streets and alleys over and over again, often photographing the same door in different light conditions and frequently wondering how I could have missed a particular door in my previous rambles.

There were other unexpected challenges. Some shopkeepers' doors were never closed, at least not during daylight hours in the months I was in San Miguel. No matter how I tried to outwit the owners, some *tiendas* opened their doors before dawn and closed them after sunset. I tried to photograph them on Sundays and national holidays or during fiestas or siestas, all to no avail. I considered asking the store owners to close their doors for a while in return for some compensation, but somehow that idea went against my scheme of capturing a real moment, and I never pursued it.

I couldn't photograph other doors I wanted to include because interminable construction obstructed them or they were blocked by cars, apparently abandoned. Once, I was forcibly restrained from taking a picture of the closed door of a bank for "security" reasons, even though that door—one of the most imposing in town—is probably photographed a dozen times a day by passing tourists. All the pictures were taken with Fujichrome 100 film and Olympus cameras with lenses ranging from 24mm to 300mm in focal length. After the first few days of shooting I usually left my tripod at home—narrow streets, the traffic and sidewalks barely wide enough for one person made using it hazardous—and relied on higher shutter speeds to overcome potential vibration problems. However, the lack of a tripod and a bubble-level challenged me more in avoiding "keystoning," the convergence of vertical lines that occurs when a camera is not held to an absolute vertical and creates the disturbing illusion of buildings falling backwards. But sometimes doors of buildings hundreds of years old had given up all relationship with exact notions of verticality anyway.

I didn't choose the doors I photographed on the basis of antiquity or, for that matter, on any other rigid basis. My selection focused on design, color and pattern. Some views are of the bizarre and some, the sublime. Some doors belong to mansions and some to stables. Because they usually lack a sign and often give conflicting street numbers, the doors only hint at what lies behind them. A freshly varnished door may be the entrance to a bakery or a funeral home, while a run-down door might lead to an artist's studio or the sybaritic retreat of a famous novelist. And because I believe details are important, I have included some photographs of doorway details that intrigued me: locks, doorknockers, house numbers and other decorative elements.

During my stay San Miguel celebrated its 450th anniversary. It was a memorable celebration, with dancing in the streets and astonishing displays of fireworks. Viva San Miguel de Allende!—and many happy returns.

HUERTAS 32

ANIMAS 43

CUADRANTE 36

CANAL 4

ARBOLES 7A

CALLEJÓN BLANCO 22

HERNÁNDEZ MACÍAS 86

HERNÁNDEZ MACÍAS 40

LORETO

CHORRO 30

SIERRA GORDA 8

HERNÁNDEZ MACÍAS 90A

JÉSUS 15

HERNÁNDEZ MACÍAS 43

CALZADA DE LA PRESA 25

INSURGENTES 75

PLAZA DE ALLENDE 14

ALTA DE LA GARITA 14

APARICIO 47

RELOJ 31

CHIQUITOS 2A

PILA SECA 29

LORETO 70

BARRANCA 38

43

LOS SUSPIROS 3A

PIEDRAS CHINAS 9

SAN JOSÉ 34

CALZADA DE LA LUZ 56

ANIMAS 3

SAN FRANCISCO 34

49

APARICIO 4

PILA SECA 3

SOLLANO 74

CALLEJÓN DE BAYONETA 8

CHORRO 26

SAN PEDRO 21

MONTES DE OCA 30

JÉSUS 44-46

INSURGENTES 155

NUÑEZ 26

MURILLO 2

CHIQUITOS 3

61

JÉSUS 32

HERNÁNDEZ MACÍAS 54

NUÑEZ 40

ZACATEROS 4

HIDALGO 32

ORTIZ 3A

CALZADA DE LA LUZ 32

CALLEJÓN CARDO

CALLEJÓN CARDO 10A

TEMPLO DE LAS MONJAS

IGLESIA DE SAN JUAN DE DIOS

ALDAMA 6

ALDAMA 2

BARRANCA 64

SAN JOSÉ 12

PILA SECA 36

RELOJ 77

SAN FRANCISCO 64

HERNÁNDEZ MACÍAS 98

SALIDA QUERÉTARO 28

PUEBLITO 5

SOLLANO 42

SOLLANO 8

CHEPITO 32

85

CUADRANTE 36

SAN FRANCISCO 20A

SAN FRANCISCO 62

HIDALGO 32

HIDALGO 21

SAN FRANCISCO 48

ALDAMA 12

HOSPICIO 5

CALLE SAN PEDRO 5

CALLE SAN PEDRO 5

SANTO DOMINGO 32

CORREJIDORA 6